Undersea Life
to Color

Green sea turtle

Illustrated by Jenny Cooper

Designed by Nelupa Hussain
Written by Susan Meredith

Most of the animals pictured in this book live among coral
reefs in the warm seas of the Indo-Pacific region.

Butterfly fish

Butterfly fish flit around in the water and many have 'eyespots', like butterflies.

The spots on their backs and tails are bigger than their real eyes. This confuses enemies and helps keep the fish safe.

Eyespot

These are copperband butterfly fish. They have copper-colored stripes.

Beak

The front stripe goes through the fish's eye.

These fish are also known as long-beaked coralfish because they have an unusually long 'beak'. They can push it into crevices to dig out food.

Sea slugs

These dazzling slugs are called variable neon sea slugs. They have bumpy green markings that are either striped or spotted.

Their 'horns' are tentacles that they use for smelling.

The slugs' sucker-like undersides help them cling to rocks.

These cabbagey-looking parts are gills that the slugs breathe through. They can be green or orange.

Striped neon sea slugs

Spotted neon sea slug

Sea squirts

The slugs absorb poison from the sea squirts they eat. They store it in their bodies, then release it in a slime if they are threatened.

Angelfish

These are regal angelfish, also known as royal, or empress, angelfish.
They got their name because of their magnificent colors and patterns.

The blue and yellow stripes on their
bodies continue onto their fins.

This fin is so dark it often
looks totally black but in
fact has blue spots.

These fish sometimes
swim upside down.

Some regal angelfish have blue-gray faces
and chests instead of yellow.

Sea dragons

Nicknamed 'leafies', leafy sea dragons like this one live off the coast of southern Australia. Despite their 'leaves', they're actually fish.

They look like floating seaweed, so enemies can't spot them. The shrimp and sea lice they eat can't see them either. They try to shelter in the dragons' 'leaves', only to be sucked up their tube-like snouts.

Snout

Sharp spine

Spines help to defend leafies against attackers.

The skin on their bodies is tough and their stripes are bony. Their 'leaves' are made of skin too.

Mandarinfish

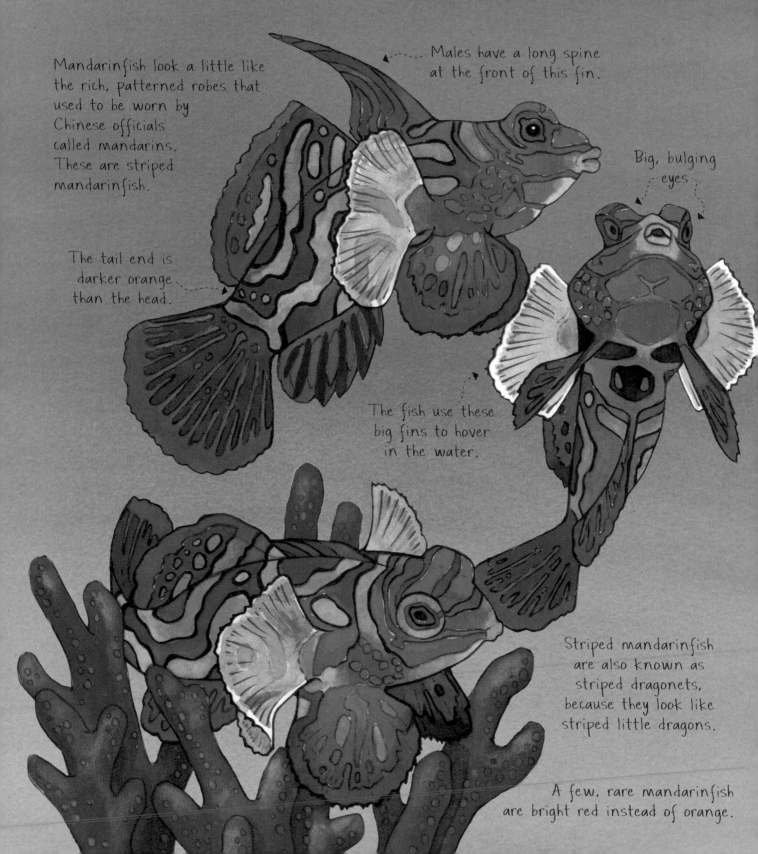

Mandarinfish look a little like the rich, patterned robes that used to be worn by Chinese officials called mandarins. These are striped mandarinfish.

Males have a long spine at the front of this fin.

Big, bulging eyes

The tail end is darker orange than the head.

The fish use these big fins to hover in the water.

Striped mandarinfish are also known as striped dragonets, because they look like striped little dragons.

A few, rare mandarinfish are bright red instead of orange.

Octopuses

Most octopuses are fairly dull-colored. This helps them hide against sand and rocks.

Even blue-ringed octopuses, like this one, normally look pale gold, but when they're disturbed, their rings glow dramatically and frighten enemies away.

Octopuses use suckers on their tentacles for touching and tasting.

Eye

Some of these rings may join together.

Octopuses use their tentacles to grab crabs and shrimp to eat, and to swim or crawl around. If they lose a tentacle, they can grow another in a couple of months.

Blue-ringed octopuses are deadly poisonous. One bite can kill a human in only a few minutes.

Rainbow wrasse

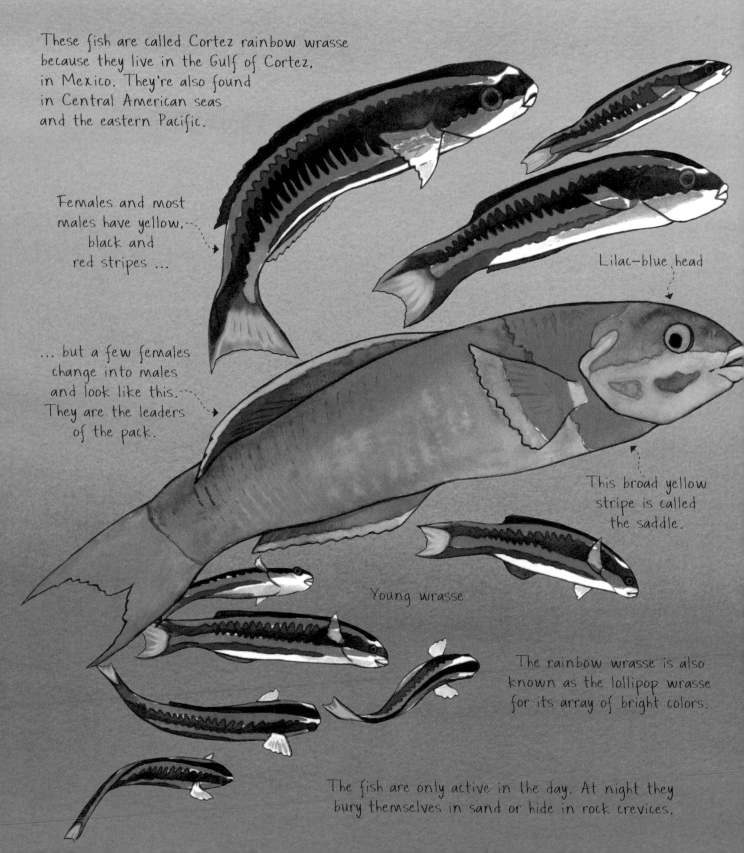

These fish are called Cortez rainbow wrasse because they live in the Gulf of Cortez, in Mexico. They're also found in Central American seas and the eastern Pacific.

Females and most males have yellow, black and red stripes ...

... but a few females change into males and look like this. They are the leaders of the pack.

Lilac-blue head

This broad yellow stripe is called the saddle.

Young wrasse

The rainbow wrasse is also known as the lollipop wrasse for its array of bright colors.

The fish are only active in the day. At night they bury themselves in sand or hide in rock crevices.

Starfish

Despite their name, starfish aren't fish and can't swim. This type is called a red-knobbed starfish because it has bright red bumps on its arms.

The bumps act like armor and help protect the starfish from attacks by fish or birds.

The stripes connecting the bumps look like a grid of wires. They are hard, like the bumps.

Suckers

Starfish cling to rocks and crawl around using hundreds of suckers on their underside.

A prickly black sea urchin

Red-knobbed starfish are also known as red-spined starfish.

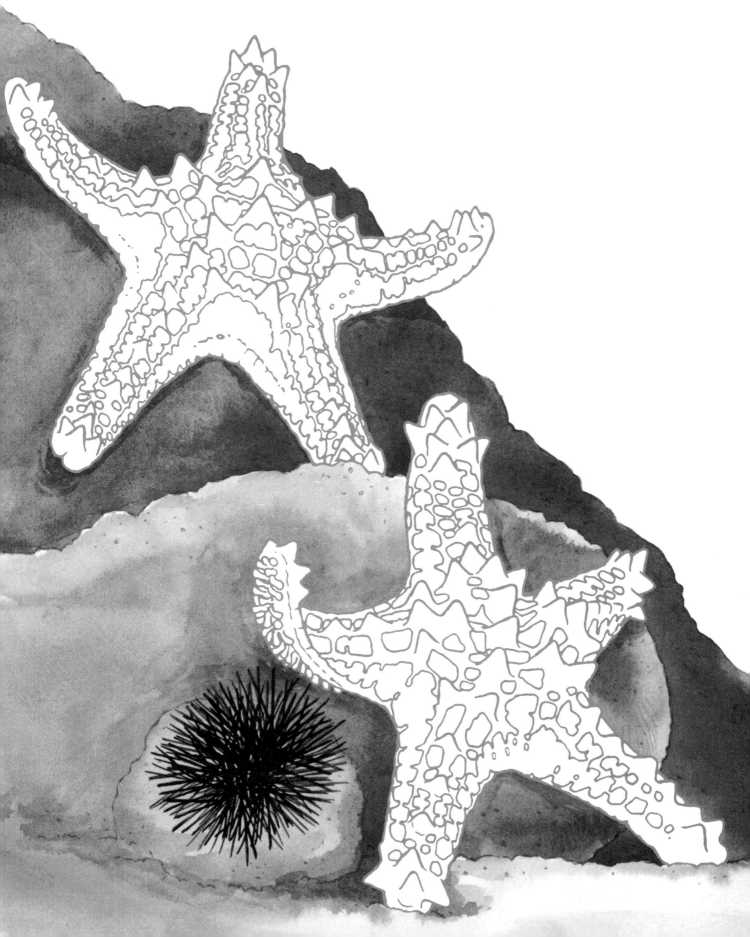

Eels

Eels are long, snakelike fish. This type is called a blue ribbon eel – its long, flat body makes it look like a ribbon when it's swimming.

The eels hide in sandy burrows or in rocks, darting out to feed on small, passing fish.

They look fierce, with their gaping jaws, but they have to keep their mouths open to breath.

The eels swim using this yellow fin which runs the length of their bodies.

Flat body

Big fin

Tiny fin

They have huge nostrils that fan out at the end. They use them to sniff out food.

These 'barbels' help them to feel their way around.

Lionfish

These 'red' lionfish live along the east coast of America and in the Caribbean, as well as the Indo-Pacific region.

They are among the most deadly fish in the world. Their fins look feathery, but have sharp, poisonous spines that the fish use to stab attackers.

Some fins have brown stripes .....

... and others have black dots.

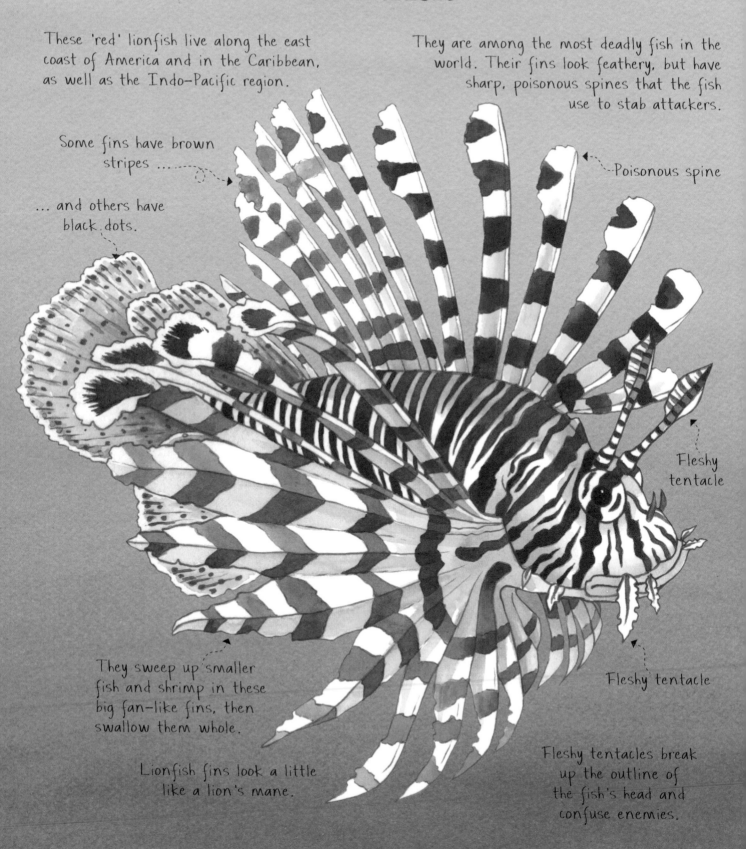

Poisonous spine

Fleshy tentacle

They sweep up smaller fish and shrimp in these big fan-like fins, then swallow them whole.

Lionfish fins look a little like a lion's mane.

Fleshy tentacle

Fleshy tentacles break up the outline of the fish's head and confuse enemies.

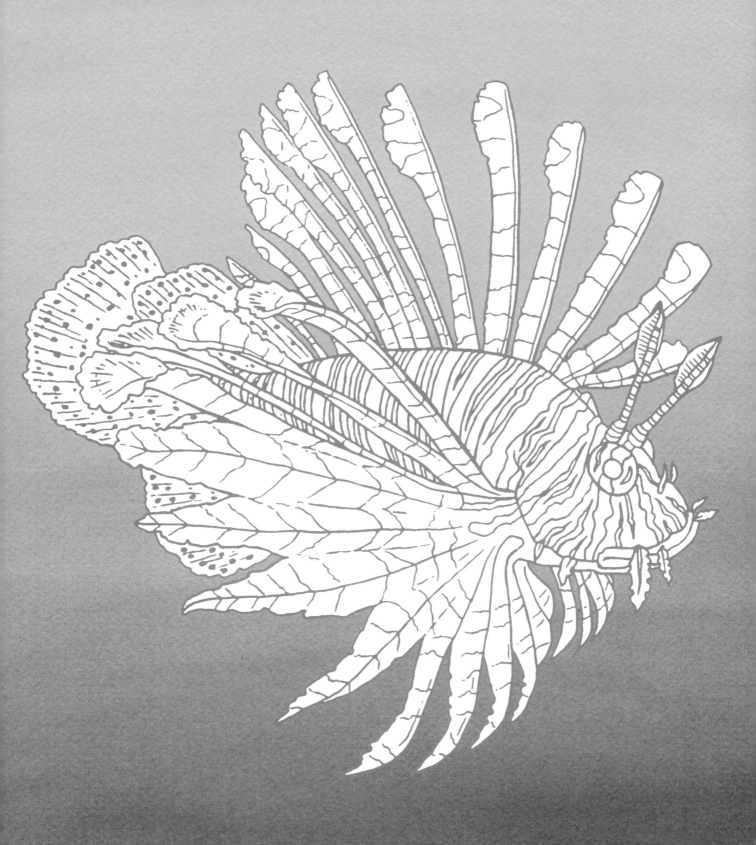

More sea slugs

All sea slugs have soft bodies that are easily damaged but the vibrant colors of these kuniei (pronounced koo-nee-eye) startle enemies away. Their skin is poisonous.

The shimmery, upper part is called a mantle, because it forms a cloak over the slug's underbody. It ripples as the slug moves.

Kuniei breathe through these plume-like gills at the back of their bodies.

They use these horn-like tentacles for sniffing out sponges, which are their favorite food.

Soft underbody

Sea turtles

Sea turtles are among the oldest creatures on Earth and live in many of the world's seas.

These are green sea turtles. They have a layer of green fat underneath their shells although you can't see it.

Yellow tang fish help to keep turtles' shells clean by eating the algae that grow on them.

Unlike other turtles, sea turtles can't pull their heads into their shells.

Green sea turtles eat sea grass that grows on the ocean floor.

Their legs are shaped like flippers.

More angelfish

This type of angelfish is called the emperor because of its large size and impressive pattern and colors.

A dark 'mask' hides its eyes. This confuses enemies, who can't tell which end of the fish is which, or even whether it's right-side up.

'Mask'

These little fish are jewel fairy basslets.

Adult emperor angelfish have striking blue and yellow stripes ...

... but young ones look so different that scientists used to think they were two completely different types of fish.

Young emperor angelfish

Hermit crabs

There are hundreds of types of hermit crabs. They live alone in empty shells, similar to religious men called hermits who used to live in caves.

The crabs carry their shells wherever they go and keep their soft tummies hidden safely inside.

They have two sets of bright orange antennae.

Their eyes are on long stalks which can move in all directions.

As a hermit crab grows, it needs a bigger shell. If it can't find an empty one, it kills a snail, or another crab, and steals its shell.

Eye

Antenna

Antenna

This is an electric-blue hermit crab. Its blue stripes are so vivid they look electric.

These crabs use two big green pincers to catch food, fight, and block up the shell entrance when they're resting inside it.

More mandarinfish

Spotted mandarinfish, like these, are also known as picturesque dragonets, because they look like pretty little dragons.

Their fins are striped.

Female

The long spine on this fin shows the fish is male.

Male

Mandarinfish produce a slime around themselves which helps to protect them from enemies and diseases.

The fish spend the daytime pecking around for food on coral. They swim very slowly.

Their colors fade when they're resting at night. This makes it harder for enemies to spot them.

Female

Coloring hints and tips

You can use colored pencils, felt-tip pens, or watercolor paints or pencils to color in your pictures. If you use watercolors, put a piece of cardboard under your page to keep the rest of the book dry.

Colored pencils

Colored pencils give a soft effect and are good for doing shading.

To fill in large areas, do lots of lines all going in the same direction.

In areas with shading, press firmly for the dark areas, then gradually reduce the pressure where the color gets lighter.

You can blend different colors together by shading them on top of each other.

Watercolors

Make watercolors lighter by adding more water, or darker by adding less.

For distinct colors, let one color dry before you add the next.

Wet watercolors blur together.

Felt-tip pens

For a bolder effect, without much shading, you could use felt-tips.

Use a fine-tipped pen for small or detailed areas.

With thanks to Richard Cambridge
Digital manipulation by John Russell

 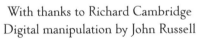